MW00475955

Evolution of the Genus Iris

Especially for

Thor & Eliza

with loving good wishes
and bushels of bright
leaves & feathers worth
of admiration — may
the poems bring a smile,
from Bob
Wild Arts
Portland
Nov

BOOKS BY ROBERT MICHAEL PYLE

PROSE

Wintergreen: Rambles in a Ravaged Land

The Thunder Tree: Lessons from an Urban Wildland

Where Bigfoot Walks: Crossing the Dark Divide

Nabokov's Butterflies (Editor, with Brian Boyd & Dmitri Nabokov)

Chasing Monarchs: Migrating with the Butterflies of Passage

Walking the High Ridge: Life as Field Trip

Sky Time in Gray's River: Living for Keeps in a Forgotten Place

Mariposa Road: The First Butterfly Big Year

Letting the Flies Out (chapbook of poems, essays & stories)

The Tangled Bank: Essays from Orion

ON ENTOMOLOGY

Watching Washington Butterflies

The Audubon Society Field Guide to North American Butterflies

The IUCN Invertebrate Red Data Book (with S. M. Wells & N. M. Collins)

Handbook for Butterfly Watchers

Butterflies: A Peterson Color-In Book (with Roger Tory Peterson & Sarah Anne Hughes)

Insects: A Peterson Field Guide Coloring Book (with Kristin Kest)

The Butterflies of Cascadia

Evolution of the *Genus* IRIS

poems by

ROBERT MICHAEL PYLE

LOST HORSE PRESS
Sandpoint, Idaho

Copyright © 2014 by Robert Michael Pyle.
Printed in America.
All Rights Reserved.

All rights reserved. No part of this book may be reproduced or transmitted in any form or by any means, electronic or mechanical, including photocopy, recording, or any information storage and retrieval system now known or to be invented, without permission in writing from the publisher, except by a reviewer who wishes to quote brief passages in connection with a review written for inclusion in a magazine, newspaper or broadcast.

Cover Art by Lexie Sundell. *Purple Fire*, acrylic on canvas, 30 x 36 inches.
    Other fine paintings by Lexi Sundell can be viewed online at *www.lexisundell.com.*
Author Photo by Benjamin Drummond, whose work may be viewed online at www.bdsjs.com.
Book & Cover Design by Christine Holbert.

FIRST EDITION

This and other Lost Horse Press titles may be viewed online at www.losthorsepress.org.

LIBRARY OF CONGRESS CATALOGING-IN-PUBLICATION DATA

Pyle, Robert Michael.
   [Poems. Selections]
   Evolution of the Genus Iris : poems / by Robert Michael Pyle.—First Edition.
      pages cm
   Includes bibliographical references.
   ISBN 978-0-9911465-4-3 (alk. paper)
   I. Title.
   PS3616.Y545A6 2014
   811'.6—dc23
                        2013045743

for Thea

and to the memory of
Howard Whetstone Pyle, *poet*

CONTENTS

What is lovelier . . . than a riverine thicket?

—Jim Harrison, "The Debtors"

I ask nothing better in the whole world than the woods.
(*Nobis placeant ante omnia silvae.*)

—Virgil, *The Eclogues*

GARDEN CATALOG

for Thea

I

Washing dishes, I look up
and there you are—turning
gray earth to brown
as you ready the garden for spring.
How do you bend like that,
so far at the waist? You shake
the clods to rid the roots of dirt
like a terrier shakes a rat.
The cat watches the stony drive
as if he expects someone to come.

You plant coneflowers, purple and white,
basil, pepper, scabiosa, echinops—
a temporary mixture, you say—
within the arch of kerria and fuchsia,
beside tomatoes mulched with grass.
On the right, perennials rise (orange
poppy, cerise foxglove, all the others);
on the left, buttercups quietly strangle
strawberries. I cannot imagine this garden
without you.

II

I like watching you bend
like that, making the soil over,
your hands black with it, my hands
warm in the dishwater. You pause,
considering which plant to plant next,
breaking it free from the black plastic cage
that held in its eager roots.

Set it into fresh-turned earth
before it drowns in evening air.
The cat turns back (no one came), pads
into the kitchen in hopes the aroma of lamb
has some basis in reality, but the dishes are done
and the lamb's all gone. So I put him out again
to help you.

AFTER BIRTH

After the mastodons, the condors ate
the afterbirths of elk,
unlucky deer in winter,
road kills.

I remember those homebirth hippies,
shared their babies' afterbirths—
the only meat, they said,
you don't have to kill.

Did those pure-hearted cannibals know
they were in the company of condors
and coyotes, famous recyclers of cats
and the afterbirths of calves?

Sweet placenta! Soil of the soul's flesh,
body bag of almost all the mammals past—
how you feed the world is your business,
cast-off as you are, after birth.

Now, slipping past my Amtrak berth
these rose hips and bramble knots,
grass-seed swards,
hazel catkins,

these widgeon, mallard, teal and grebe,
harrier, heron, kestrel, crane,
strawberries, chard, tomatoes rotting by the rails:
aren't all of these the offspring of the land?

And what shall I call these fallow fields,
this stubble, streams clouded with soil and milt,
these towns and houses crumbling into pulp
and afterbirths?

Beyond the borning
comes what's left.
Sometimes it's all there is,
leaving me to wonder—

after the condors, who will eat the leavings?
After the coyote,
after the birth of dying?

GOING DOWN AGAIN

As a man who sinks in water
I have never been gravity's friend
in open air. I remember falling—
out of a locust tree at ten, stealing
magpie eggs. Off bicycles, of course.
Hard on tailbone in the Fox Aurora, tripped
by a girl, and again on rock at Boreas Pass.
From a ladder, raking my forearm raw
on oaken bark.

Stumbling over Logan curbstone, shaking
the pavement with the force of my fall.
And once, almost over backwards
under heavy pack, on sharp pumice ridge
in the Dark Divide.

I never liked pratfalls in comedy acts. Feel
physical pain before butt meets dirt, when
it isn't even my butt. For this reason I clamber,
not climb, up mountains. For this reason,
I go slowly over broken ground.
It is good that my bones are like those
of Titanotheres, the way my body craves
the earth.

Yesterday in Billy Meadows, my foot found
a stick end-on. "Pole vault" came to mind
as I shot up, out, and down. Landed
on cheek with crack! I took for bone, or lens
at least. Lay there, taking stock. Then, daubing
a little blood, stood, and shook it off.
Happy, *happy*, to be back up,
one more time.

THE GRIEF OF THRUSHES

When I saw the brown lump still between the gray cat's paws
I took it for a Townsend's vole—one of those great cat sausages,
their tunnels so hard on the garden. Take the voles, we say,
and be content; leave their gall bladders big as marbles for us, and leave
the flying squirrels, the jumping mice, and all the birds alone.
But this was no vole. It lay compliant, but alive, struggling
just a little. Cupped in my hands, it seemed a sparrow, but the bill
said thrush. *Oh, kitty!* Not the Swainson's, who come in May
and make of June evenings a madrigal of whistle, chitter,
and tumbling trill—not one of theirs!

But it was. And here's the bad part: the mother. The whole time I held
her young, she flew 'round and 'round the wood, calling,
calling. That piping plaint carried on into dark, 'round and 'round,
long after I placed the chick on a pile of leaves. Its bill opened
in silent answer, one leg dangling, one wing stretching. Then it died,
as the cat looked around in disgrace. Never mind
her partial exculpation: discovery of downy feathers
where the bird hit the window before the pounce.
In the morning, eyes gone, snail's streak shimmering
over wing, still the mother circled, and called.

Just as I wonder, in an old graveyard serried with stones
of one, two, five, six-year olds, how the parents stood it,
so too with birds: just a momentary itch of absence
would be the merciful thing, most of their young taken
by cat or crow or coon. But who knows? If you'd flown
10,000 miles, found a mate, fashioned a nest, hunted down
10,000 caterpillars, only to lose it all to a cat at fledging,
maybe you too would circle and keen, circle and keen.

HORSEBACK AT DAWN

for Gary Nabhan and Ofelia Zepeda

The night before, in a John Wayne western,
we watched black-and-white Indians chase
the stage coach, as bullets flew and the same
stone towers rolled past again and again.

Up at five, and there they were: those towers,
in color, standing still, and the Indians too.
Navajos met us at the stable: Harold the albino
trail boss, Ron and Alex the wranglers.
They took half an hour to lasso and saddle
the little Indian ponies, tough and matty.
Then we rode into the silence
of the red rocks. A little way on

Harold said "Now you guys got to take
your imagination out of your back pocket."
And then he said, "Now let's gallop!"
It was all my imagination could do
to keep me in the saddle when I yelled "Whoa!"
and my once-white pony whoa'd on a dime. She
was named Edge, and I named my bruises
the Edge Effect. At the end of how far we could go,

Harold said "Now you guys get to hear a prayer."
He and Alex sang a Navajo chant that I hoped
would cover the return trip, while Raven looped
a slow ink scrawl overhead. Going back I did not yell.
The towers ran by again, and the Indians surrounded us,
just like in the movie.

But no one was shooting,
and only the ponies, barn-sour,
were running away.

SILAGE

for Bobby Larson

Writing letters on a January day
I miss the silage. Its sour stink
riding on the fog like a front man for rot,
its leaking heaps, seething
beneath winter blankets of black plastic.

"Green chop" is what they call the cut
served straight up, field to cud
without benefit of bales. Next comes hay, baked
dry and sweet by autumn's breath to greet
damp muzzles with rumors of summer.

Finally, silage: no fresh fodder,
these ammoniac mounds, these foetid sediments.
But magic, how bacteria's touch
makes milk from sodden veg,
months from any meadow.

When the dairy herds left,
so went silage, and its reek
like a needle to the nose that shouts
this is the land, *this* is real,
as clear as any of this valley's voices.

Oh yes, I miss the silage. Just look
how I try to make my own
from these neglected letters, composting
correspondence. If only I could feed it
to the cows. If only I could smell it.

"RARE WORM DOESN'T SPIT OR SMELL SWEET"

Thus spake *USA Today* when
the Palouse Giant Earthworm
turned up again after twenty years
of absence. Well, not really *absence*.
They were down there all along,
relaxing into their flaccid longitude,
deep underground. Their cousins,
the Oregon Giant Earthworms, had
been missing even longer.

Old lore said the Palouse Giant
Earthworm smells like lilies. Old
lore said it spits, and stretches
up to six feet long. Not so,
said *USA Today*—these were only
foot-longs, no spit, no sweet scent.
Kind of like finding Bigfoot, and he's
only five-foot-ten, with 9B trotters.

I don't know about the spitting. But
what if you were lost for twenty years,
then found, and weren't the same
as everyone expected? What if
they all found out
you don't smell like lilies
after all?

PINK PAVEMENTS

How the sidewalks flush and run
when cherries, crabs, and apples shed
their petal pelts. How exploded
blossoms soften concrete and stone.

In Colorado, nights before track meets,
I walked and walked, dreaming of Olympus,
holding in the exhalations of Hopa crabs
that lined our streets. Next day, the same cold
wind that always blew my discus down too soon
would strew the streets with pale pink disks.

In Cambridge, cherry blossoms daubed
the rosy fronts of colleges, scented stale
doorways of pubs. Memories of winter on harsh
fen breath stripped set fruits of flower, laid
pink silk over ancient pavements, lifting skirts
and dressing lanes in time for the May Balls.

Even now, when hard spring wind unclothes
the cherries in town and crabapples thicken
the night air, I feel the blunt rim of the discus
on my fingers, the cool rim of the pint on my lips.
And I think, as yet another April whiles itself
away in war,

how the pavements of Baghdad must go pink,
spattered with the petals of peaches and plums,
when the car bombs burst. How blossoms
soften exploded concrete and bone.

HEARTH

for Bilak Bokis

When the fat black cat
plants his sleek self
on the round blue rug
beneath the hot blue stove
he anchors this home
to the earth.

DANCING PANTS

The blue cotton panties
and white cotton briefs
dance
in the warm air
of the heat vent, swing
back and forth, up and down,
on drying rack bars.
Perpetual motion
in the nether regions,
tireless.
Don't their owners wish
their pants would always dance like that,
at the mere lick
of hot breath?

EARLY MORNING IN WYOMING

Three tall, slender sisters climb down from the cab
of a pick-up pulling a horse box. They wear
ball caps, two red, one brown, over long
braids. Moving smoothly in form-fitting wool,
willowy and shy, barely notice the old-timer
waking up in his jalopy. Offload
two chestnuts and a gray, lead them onto the range,
run them in circles by their bridles to warm them up.
Then, two bareback, one saddled, they mount.

Shyness shed, self-possessed on horseback, trot
over the ridge, blonde braids flying,
border collies bouncing. Disappear
into the sage: three female centaurs,
loping off to do something ancient
with dogs and cattle.

LIFE AND DEATH IN YELLOWSTONE

I Buffaloed at the Black Dragon

At dusk the mud volcanoes belch
sardonic insults at the tawny-rocked park.
Walking to Black Dragon's Cauldron, I think
life could begin here, in the sulfurous roil.
Ill-mannered yammerers arrive, and I throw
them in. Or want to (sinking, then silent in the boiling
goo), but I have mercy. "Warning!" says the sign:
"people have been scalded to death! Unstable
crust, don't leave trail." Don't yammer,
I add—life could end here too.

I sense something behind me, turn to see Bison,
like the Black Dragon arisen from its cauldron.
Grazing above the simmering pool it stands black-
shaggy, huge-headed, devil-horned, wicked-loined.

II Eagle-Eyed at Artist's Point

Tuffy walls split by the first Atlantic spume
like the greatest nether cleft there ever was—
enflamed flesh, engorged orange, impassioned pink—
pilose with junipers, hirsute with firs.
You can see the canyon-maker gush
like the greatest spurt there ever was.
These genitive events were long ago,
volcanoes and glaciers now gone flaccid
to the point of absence.

I can see why Moran and Bierstadt came
—their canvases, their glossy old oils—
some kind of sorcery. I can see the hocus-pocus
as an eagle, mantle flashing golden off a minaret,
takes wing, and huge among the swallows' motes,
becomes a red-tailed hawk.

III *Blowing Kisses to Yellowstone*

At Old Faithful I boarded the Baptists' bus,
grabbed the mike and gave them hell
for spouting silly songs that stole
the famous gusher's moment.

And there was the time I watched Terry,
my gymnast friend, pull a handstand on the rail
above the yawning gorge, as a woman watching
aghast croaked, "Damn you!"

Once upon West Thumb I camped
in empty autumn, awoke to snow. Perfect
for prowling the lonesome park,
but the greedy highway heisted the day.

"We're always blowing kisses to Yellowstone,"
you said. Now, every time I see the Tetons
poking over Togwotee, I hope for more
than just postcards of steam and creatures.

THE BUTTERFLIES OF BILLY MEADOWS

First, of course, the swallowtails catch the eye:
Papilio zelicaon, rutulus, multicaudatus,
and *Parnassius smintheus,* Apollo's alter ego.
Then the whites flit by: *Pieris occidentalis*
and *Pieris rapae,* cabbage butterflies even here.
Anthocharis sara with her orange-juice tips,
and the butterpats of sulphurs: *Colias interior,*
their bright pink edges, their lime-green eyes.

Of the blues, *Euphilotes* occupy the buckwheat
mounds, *Icaricia* the lupine, named for *Icarus,*
that wax-winged wannabe. *Plebejus saepiolus,*
greenish blue; *Plebejus lupini,* spangled blue.
And *Glaucopsyche*—that means blue soul!—*piasus*
and *lygdamus,* the arrowhead and silvery blues.
Pyrgus communis, skipping on checkered wings,
just looks blue. *Lycaena heteronea* shines bluer
than any blue, though it's really a copper—like
mariposa flashing purple in the sun, *nivalis* of the
lilac edge, or Edith's, named for her finder's lover.

And the browns: *Cercyonis pegala* and *oetus*—O,
ye Wood Nymphs of Summer! Plus their fair sister,
Erebia epipsodea, flitting cinnamon and chocolate
through alpine hellebores by Billy Creek. *Boloria
epithore,* violet and rust, in bog with Ochre Ringlets.
Vanessa the Lady flies by, like a cinder on the wind;
Erynnis the witch, black as a burned-out coal. The
anglewing known here as Zephyr; the tortoiseshell
of fiery rims; and blue-flecked Antiopa, the Mourning
Cloak—all brilliant above, all hide behind dark rags.

Look, here come the checkerspots and crescents!
Phyciodes mylitta and *pulchella* "the beauty";
Euphydryas "(lovely dryad") *colon*, and *E. anicia*
veaziae, named for Portland dryad Agnes Veazie,
who caught Oregon silverspots in Ocean Park in '16.
Now, all these silverspots at their violets: *Speyeria*
hydaspe, callippe, zerene, coronis, hesperis, leto,
and *mormonia*: one pair of Mormon Fritillaries,
in copula, of course. Lastly, at Buckhorn Lookout,
Danaus plexippus—one lone Monarch, beating
its way back north, high above Imnaha.

BOTANY LESSON: CLEOME

for Ann Zwinger

He called it bee balm, but I heard bee bomb.
Ray worked graveyard at Gates Rubber, spent
summer mornings collecting in the canyons west
of town. When he took me along, we'd leap
from his Rambler by Turkey Creek, creep
up on the bee bomb, swing our nets,
and hoot with glee.

Riding back to Denver, both of us nodding off,
I'd see what our sweep had erased: butterflies—
mole-brown, coral-spotted, thrilling, drunk
on the nectar of those purple flowers
that the field guides call *Cleome.*

Tame Cleome nods in ghetto gardens,
springs from city flowerbeds: pale versions,
long-legged, pink-and-ivory spiders perched
on tall green stalks. I'd almost forgotten

the wild ones until La Baca, when lovers
of land and language, escaping words, walked
the lap of a western range. Sandy flats bloomed
lavender like smoke, and Alamosa wood nymphs
spread Cleome's pollen.

Theophrastus of Rome had a mustard in mind
when he coined "Cleome" in Latin. Ray too mixed up
the name: real bee balm's a mint named *Monarda,*
while *Cleome*'s a caper called spider plant, or bee
plant, for the love of honeybees—but never bee balm.

Even still: as long as butterflies haunt
these explosions of nectar and scent
and I can hear that Polish rubber-worker's
laugh above the taunts of Turkey Creek,
it will always be bee bomb to me.

DIP-TYCH

I like butterflies
quite a lot. But flies
(minus the butter) abound,
and few folks notice
except to swat.
Take a good look sometime:
you'll see they are beautiful
and do lots of neat things
that few even see. Butter-
flies come and go but
flies just come and come and come.
Some look just like wasps,
others like furry bumblebees.
Some have antlers!
Some shimmer blue, some have eyes
like rainbows. Everyone
loves butterflies. But what about
flies? And so much discovery
to be made! Sometimes I think
instead of a Lepi 'dopterist,
I should have been

a dipterist.

RELEASING THE HORSEFLIES

Every day I visit the half-screened
back porch to let the horseflies
out. Smart enough to get in,
too dumb to get out, they wham!
against the rusty screen
all day long.

The horseflies are big and slow and easy
to catch and toss out. The hover flies,
passive and happy to go. The smaller ones
have to fend for themselves. I need a glass
for the bumblebees.

Why release horseflies, anyway? Well,
they're no skin off my nose, or arm, or neck,
if I watch out. Besides, I can't stand
frustration in any animal,
and a big fly battering a screen
is the very definition of frustration.

And, oh! their stripéd silken eyes
are beautiful.

NEWS ITEM

When the twister came, it ripped the seal
clean out of the Tennessee state flag.
"Just a big red flag with a hole in the middle,"
said an observer, "like a cannonball
went right through it." Still flying,
waving red against the roiled sky. But blue,
where the seal should have been.

There are people whose clothes blow
in the wind like that, arms and legs in motion
as if everything is A-OK. But when you look
closely, their hearts are missing. Blown away;
cannonball-gone.

You can see right through.

WHEN ONCE IN MOUNT ST. HELENS' LAP

When Vaux's swifts propel from snag
to Meta Lake's clear air and snatch
the morning's hatch of bronze-back caddis,
nighthawks slice the pink-steam dusk, mouth
the moths that come to firelight. When checkerspots
cruise the pumice heights for nectar brewed
from ash by penstemon and pussypaws. When
meadowrue and *Montia*, valerian and saxifrage,
cow parsnip, goatsbeard, *Oplopanax horridum*
all leap from sheltering ledge with scents
that sweeten death and whites that mirror
pallor of the floating forest down below,
they make all that dying into art. Three ravens
saunter past to say it's so.

When barn swallows scream and struggle
toward their nest on Windy Ridge, rough-
winged swallows ride Green River's slot.
When Lorquin's admiral seals her eggs
on willow leaves above the falling wall,
then glides the rim where buckwheat feeds
the butterfly whose wings turn UV indigo.

When Sitka alder, noble fir, and western hemlock,
hazel, black cottonwood, and silver fir all *spring*
out of tefra, raising forest in their own sweet time,
and six different wintergreens freshen blasted woods,
and *Usnea* lichen, *Racomitrium* moss, brown bolete
and yellow slime mold all *travel*
at their own chosen speeds. When western toad
and long-horned beetle hold the ground down
and a tiny white spot in a hole in the sky, when glassed
becomes a sun-struck spider a hundred feet up,
orb strung across the canopy gap in the roof
of Douglas-fir. When lupine and paintbrush, daisy

and hawkbit and pearly everlasting all *cloak*
the popcorn rocks, where bumblebees come
to conspire with petal and pollen,
and sedges blow heavy in the wind—then I know
that when Loo Wit blew up,
all these
are what came out.

LULLABY FOR PATTIANN

East Fork of the Lewis River

Friend, while you wait for all those angels
or incubi to tug at your compliant gown

And till the perfect morning dawns
for dewy rolling in the nude

And prior to appearance of naked boys
on naked ponies alongside your very own Beagle

And while you're watching for that hummingbird's
plummet, pinfeathers dripping on your behalf . . .

In the meantime: I hope you'll exult to randy
ravens, jumping each other's hollow bones on high

Thrill in your blood to the elderberry bursting
rank green from dry and brittle branches

Share the violet surprise as pasqueflower erupts
past dry brown needles of ponderosa pine

Grab the whole sweet obscenity of spring
as sleep and sap trade places.

For the tree frogs and the peat bogs love their love
and rot and row and jelly-belly amplitude in March,

When disquiet upsets everyone, and rest
comes only with satiety. Furthermore I hope

While you're waiting for the news today
that only you can hear,

The towhee's scree will lull you
like the very voice of angels.

THE OTHER SIDE OF SILENCE

If we had a keen vision and feeling of all ordinary human life,
it would be like hearing the grass grow and the squirrel's heart beat,
and we should die of that roar which lies on the other side of silence.

—George Eliot, *Middlemarch*

It has to be one of the finest phrases
in all of English, this name of Eliot's
for a place so few of us have ever been.

I'd like to think it was somewhere
one could choose to go, like
booking a ticket to Chicago, or Boise.

But what if you got there, and hated it?
What if the other side of silence
was a muscle car pulling onto the beach
approach with hip-hop on the woofers?

But, no. I think it would be like winter
wren turning off in a green shade; like
the voice of Venus over the cold Pacific.

Like peace itself: that state
we've barely known
on this side of silence.

COYOTE, HIT

Abject, is how that animal looked,
standing by the highway as if it couldn't think
which way to go. And when it did walk away
I saw why. From behind, against the gray.
Its gait was crooked: not a fleet trot
like *coy-o-te*,
but slow and wonky,
out of whack. Not smooth,
but syncopated. Clownish,
if it hadn't been all wrong,
hopelessly broken.

The coyote started across the road
as a dump truck came along. I feared
it wouldn't get across in time. Then saw
its left foreleg, limp and floppy,
and feared it would. I have killed
broken-backed animals with blows
to the head from blunt objects,
and a dump truck would be faster. I hoped
I wouldn't watch, and knew I would.

But the possibility of mercy on huge wheels passed,
and coyote crossed, that paw dangling
like a dead vole worried from the ground
and carried home to pups. It turned,
lay down in wet grass by the cold hearth
of the verge. Its sodden pelt, that soft
and muddy everycolored cape, prickly,
rain-streaked, stood on end.

It watched me, as I drove away.

BLUES

In the summer of nineteen seventy-six,
by reflecting pool for Lincoln's monument,
metallic blue wings shone like Superman's hair:
a butterfly, Red-spotted Purple, basking
on the hot marble rim.

In the spring of nineteen ninety-six
—same sun, same pool, other side—
shimmering wings again shot blue:
jays, nesting in the pale green elm,
tussling over Kleenex.

Iridescent indigo, beamed
from bird to butterfly
across the decades,
across the water with its picture
of a penny's flip-side struck in white.

And here's what has changed
in twenty year's time: beyond
the placid pool has grown a wall,
long, black, and graven with names
of fifty-eight thousand twenty-two dead.

ANONYMOUS MEATS

is what he called them. Cuts
piled on the back of a barrow
that offer no clue of what or
where from. Those leering pigs'
heads in the mercado, Guadalajara;
that flensed cow's face in Angangueo.
This airplane lunch. Or roadkill,
beyond recognition by anyone
but scavengers
who don't ask names.

ALL THINGS CONSIDERED

Two river otters fished the Salmon,
diving and rising side by side, almost
down to the surf. Watching
their sleek and pointy loop-de-loop,
over and over and over,
I managed to miss
the evening news.

THE GOATS OF TAJIKISTAN

I Into Varzob

Beneath the snowy peaks of Varzob
dachas of stone and glass follow
the browning sycamores upstream
until the canyon narrows into solitude.
Across the near ridge, rock softens
to a cushion of ground grass and pellets.
Five shaggy goats—gray, black, brown,
rust, and off-off-white—pick their way
over turf they've trodden, grazed, and shat
into recycled fiber forever. They know
their way to where the valley opens out
to a tiny farm with russet fruit trees
and the goatherd's mud hut. This too
has been the same
since prophets walked the land.

A great boulder, split down the middle, crops
the white mountains, the blue sky,
like a strip torn from a photograph. I enter
the cleft, step into the heart of Varzob.
Sun silvers the rim above with backlit lichen,
moss, webs, and stalks of grass. Below
the slit lies the midden of a dormouse,
shells of walnut and pistachio. I hear
the stream below, the crows above,
rock buntings, hawfinches chipping
in yellow hawthorns—then nothing.

The goats have climbed a distant ridge.
I step out, and a brimstone butterfly zips
up that crack in the middle of Asia.

II South of Dushanbe

Beside the ruined fort at Hisor
people picnic, play soccer, visit
dark rooms of Medreseh-turned-museum
to see plows and pots and churns and swords.
Our guide tells of the old spring that watered
the mosque and fort in ancient times. "The water,"
he says, "is still pure."

An old man in Tajik cap and green velvet coat
sits atop a dusty knoll. He wants to tell
stories in exchange for an ear, a simoni or two,
but I've had enough history and excuse myself
to wander. At the spring,
brown sheep with long Nubian noses
and broad butts and pygmy goats
with curly horns and turned-up tails all bleat
and bah and browse the lush watercress
like noisy salad. A nameless rodent shoves
soil out a hole in the bank, shows tiny feet
and pink snout for a second, then disappears
beneath the ancient earth.

Children laugh and scamper to the outlet,
take turns filling plastic water bottles
downstream
from all the animals they'd chased
around green remnants of an age.
Then run back up the rutted hill
clutching their flagons of life, as
small fishes and bubbles worry
the cool water of the spring, and the sheep
and the goats chomp and cough their way
across the tired old oasis.

Long spider-strands balloon
across the arid air. Beneath that silken sky,
flutes and drums and car horns echo
frantic wedding parties out beyond
the fortress gate. The strands congeal
into silver skeins, as if veils and scarves
escaped all the brides posing for pictures,
and took off flying down the Silk Road,
somewhere south of Dushanbe.

TRUE STORY

At a rest area east of Coeur d'Alene
I bend to fetch a cluster of long pine
needles—great green spray
of ponderosa—for the smell.
But the twig is hooked on,
plugged in, held fast. Turns out
it's a bunch of Idaho fescue,
grass still green in January.

A little farther down the trail,
I stoop to stroke the soft floss
of fescue—generous fountain
of fine green blades—for the feel.
But the bunchgrass comes away in my hand,
unplugged, uprooted. Turns out
it's a sprig of ponderosa,
fallen from a bough in the wind.

LIFE CAN BE LIKE THIS SOMETIMES

Sitting in Discount Tire in Albuquerque
for your second pair of tires in a month,
steel belts showing through because
your struts are shot on an endless road trip,
thousands of miles of interstate behind
and you have to be in Long Beach tomorrow.

Or,

Chin-deep in Florida blackwater river,
alligators at bay as far as you know, swallowtails
dripping from azaleas overhead and swallow-tailed
kites over them, pileated and red-belly hooting
and yaffling their woodpecker songs,
and you with no place else to be in a hurry.

Take your pick.

GULLS AT REST

On the bridge lie gray lumps like so many
dust-bunnies blowing in the wakes of trucks,
plucked and pummeled by the river wind.
From the span's high deck you see their wraiths
rising in the morning sun from sandbar humps:
divots from the dredge's work, haunted by fogs
and damps escaping river mud, too light to stay
behind.

Every drain-hole clogged with grass, like so many
green muffs. How the wind howls through,
how the spindrift catches in those stranded
turves. All above the rails the gulls float past,
sickle-wristed, playing with the wind, eyeing
Desdemona sands for stranded clams and fish. Lighter
than the river-wraiths, too light to fall
below.

It's the young gray gulls that go down,
missing the practiced flick of wing that tips
a weightless body away from death. Gray
tumps of feather and bone that blow
away in time, fertilize the drain-hole grass, settle
into mizzling rain and rising wraiths, but never blend
with bridge. Too heavy to live, too light to fly
any more.

TWO HAIKU FROM RYUKYU

(with Gary Snyder; prose note by R. M. Pyle)

It happened like this. In March 2003, convened by Professor Katsunori Yamazato and his colleague Shin Yamashiro, the Japanese chapter of the Association for the Study of Literature and the Environment met at the University of the Ryukyus in Nishihara, Okinawa. Many scholars and writers from several Asian countries met to discuss topics in ecocriticism. A student of Terry Tempest Williams from Hiroshima, several Thoreau specialists, Rachel Carson's Japanese translator, a radical Ryukyu novelist, naturalists from Taiwan and Hokkaido and others gathered out of love of literature and land. Gary Snyder was the featured guest. The rest of the U.S. group consisted of Scott Slovic and Cheryll Glotfelty of the University of Nevada at Reno, their graduate student Ayano Ginoza (who was returning to her home in Okinawa), and myself. One of the most affecting talks for me was delivered by the Korean poet Ko Un. When he suggested that we would never find a way through all the tensions in East Asia or the world until we adopted a collective posture of *minimum ownership,* he knocked my socks off.

During breaks in the proceedings I birded around Naha, guided by an essay Gary Snyder had written after earlier visits to the Okinawan capital. I wandered ancient cobbled trackways and watery parks on the trail of brown thrushes hopping along the banks beside a historic teahouse. Post-war buildings were rendered venerable by a small leaved, clinging fig (*Ficus pumila*) that softened all the pastel, concrete walls erected after the old city was razed by bombs. But the main field trip took us beyond the city gates. We all piled onto a bus and headed south to visit a series of historic and natural places. Our first destination, Sefa Utaki, is the foremost of seven major *utaki* (sacred sites) made by the creator Amamikiyo in the Okinawan creation myth. When you duck through a triangular aperture between two giant rocks in a raised coral cliff, you come to an intimate space opening onto the western seas. Here, you can view or send prayers to the sacred Kudaka Jima (Kudaka Island), where millet and wheat first came ashore, an important event in the genesis of the Ryukyu kingdom.

Gary Snyder was attentive and quiet here at Sefa Utaki; reverent, I'd say. But when we bussed to a secular site, an old castle ruin named Chinen Jyoseki, he became more voluble. After TV reporters finished interviewing him, he made a getaway. I was birding from the shore nearby, when Gary approached and asked,

"What are you glassing, Robert?"

"I'm looking at a gray heron, Gary," I said, "out there on that tump of coral."

"Aha," he said, accepting my binoculars for a look.

Handing them back, he grinned, then recited an extemporaneous verse. Though I doubt he intended any more weight for those words than the breeze off the sea might carry, it seemed a pity to let them fly away unrecorded. Feeling more than a little Boswellian, I picked up a big, rounded leaf curing at the foot of a small tree, took out my fountain pen, and printed Gary's lines on half of the leaf. Then I added a reply on the other half and handed it to Gary-san, who chuckled. I pressed the leaf in a book and forgot about it.

A few days later, several of us were departing on our separate flights from Osaka. Ko Un was one of these, embarking for Seoul. I wanted to acknowledge my pleasure in meeting him and to thank him for his stunning words. Realizing that the gesture would only interfere with his own efforts at minimum ownership, I gave him my reading copy of *Where Bigfoot Walks*—the text I'd read from at the conference, since it had been published in a Japanese edition.

Then long after everyone was aloft, it hit me: That was the book into which I'd tucked the leaf! Oh, well, I thought—Korea's as good a destination as any for an ephemeral conversation over an Asian heron.

But later I found myself wishing I had those lines. When I learned that Ko Un's wife, Sang-Wha Lee, was a professor of English, I wrote to ask her whether she might transcribe them for me. My query was apparently lost to the ether. Since I didn't hear back for some time I wrote again and promptly received a charming note—and the haiku you see printed here.

> From the old Castle wall
> A gray heron
> And tourist buses
>
> —GS

> On the mushroom coral rock
> A gray heron
> Just sits and sits
>
> —RMP

HAIKU FOR A BEETLE WITH SPIDERWEBS ON ITS ANTENNAE

for Bill Yake, who noticed it

O polka-dotted longhorn
how did those spiderwebs
get there, anyway?

Gossamer beams across
segmented spars—which
came first? Did the spider

spin from pole to pole,
or did you merely walk
into her web?

Maybe a spiderlet ballooned
caught on long Silk Road:
one arm West, one East.

Silk strands between antennae:
do they really improve
your reception?

But what I really
want to know
is the installation cost.

swarmed up the tidal sloughs, burrowed into pothole mud behind the shore's berm. One big female, like a brown '54 Hudson, lay on her back, turned over by a kid from the local transient camp. Her great spike tail prodded like a pike seeking purchase in the sky; her eggs rolled among the billions of green BB's feeding the shorebird legions.

The Jersey kid looked up at me and asked, "Man, where's their pussy? Which one's got the dick?"

"That one's the female," I said. "She drops her eggs in the sand and the male spreads his sperms on top."

"The big one's the female?" he asked, amazed. "And they don't fuck?" He looked back at the flailing fossils. "That's fucked up, man," he said. "That ain't right."

IF HUMANS HAD SPERMATOPHORES

If humans had spermatophores
zygotes would be zip-locked,
gametes gift-wrapped, chromosomes
contained in shrink-wrapped valentines.

If germ cells merged this way,
sperms delivered in packets of promise
brighter than anything from Burpee's,
it would be impossible to spill your seed.

If men made spermatophores when they shot
their wad, there would be no wet spot on the bed.
Rubbers would be redundant, since
cum would come in cellophane.

If love arrived in shiny bubbles,
prizes packed in sheer balloons,
genes seeking genes would ply
the deeps in silken submarines.

And birth? That would be
a burst of butterflies.

ALL FALL DOWN

I

Across the valley floor rises
a broken pillar of smoke, rain-gray and pink,
congeals with low fog, smears
it a little browner than the cloud bank,
as if the sky put down December's foot
to tamp the fire, the smoky fire
in the sodden heap of all that's left
of Chamberlain's barn. Orange flickers
at its feet, scraping the remnants
of the newcomer's bales, stacked too heavy
in a loft fit only for loose hay. The straw
that broke this barn's back was gold.

Eagle flies over covered bridge, across
the distant plume. One more old one down,
one more cloud in the sky, in a land
where clouds are cheap,
and the barns are going fast.

II

Along the river shore lies
a forest of boards, salmon-red and brown,
bobbing on the high gray tide, soaking
them a little darker than their faded state,
as if the river splintered into kindling
to feed the fire, the cold fire
of the flotsam with all that's left
of Altoona Cannery. Waves flap
at its wreckage, slapping the remnants
of broad floors whose pilings gave way
when the land's loose logs came down. The flood
that took this house of salmon was time.

A wedge of geese flies over Megler Bridge, across
the far reach. One more old one down,
one more forest to the sea, in a land
where the sea is cheap
and all the rest is long gone.

THE BANANA SLUG ON THE TOTEM POLE

sits atop the heap, above coyote,
jay, and raven. All four tentacles
poke like pigtails from its head,
beside the rasping mouth,
long ones watching,
short ones sniffing,
all four palping the heady air
at such an elevation.

For such a creature of the ground
to find itself so far aloft, peering
over evolutionary betters down below,
must be a rare and pleasant perch.

Maybe not the first banana slug
that's ever crowned a pole in totem
times. But maybe it's the only one
ever carved of cedar log,
no slime trail left behind to show
how it got way up there.

THE PULASKI ON THE FLAG POLE

What's that on top of the flagpole, anyway?
Upright handle, double blades at right angles—
why, it's a Pulaski! Firefighters' tool,
one end axe, one adze,
handle of the type they call "fawn's foot."
To fell a burning snag, split a smoldering
old log, cut out a root, nothing as versatile,
nothing else serves half as well.

Gary Snyder says the most important
thing (and maybe the hardest too) is to know
your own proper work. One thing G. S. knows
is his way around the woods, another
is this tool that Ranger Ed Pulaski made
a hundred years ago. Wouldn't they both grin
at this buck-toothed salute?

No one looks for the flag that flew
over Billy Meadows Guard Station,
no one runs anything up that old pole,
but notes a damn fine tool up there. Lashed
to the top by someone who knew
his own true work all right, and knew
its worth as well.

IN CHINA

I Poem for a Panda

Good and scruffy, yellow-white dirty black, radio collar
'round its neck. Not one of those white-washed, boot-blacked,
scrubbed-and-blow-dried zoo pandas named Pei-Pei or Mei-Mei.
We hike. We wait. When Head Tracker Liang gives the word,
we follow up into thick bamboo, and there it is: crunching
shoots with great big teeth, scratching an itch
with bigger claws. Joyce sits near, like some
acolyte of Jane Goodall, like some young
woman in love with her primate of choice, till
it ups and walks away.

Later someone asks Liang how many pandas live in Foping.
"One-hundred fifteen," he says. "Not all have collars."
Trackers find bears by sign, check in with cell phones.
When they have one fit to visit, we take turns, scramble
into the forest, into the presence—
if we're fast, and lucky.

That night Mr. Wei says, "You saw that bear? He is my special study!
Collar four, name Can Can. Means 'bright.' Hundred kilograms now,
with bamboo shoots. Less when he must eat leaves. Home range: five
kilometers, or seven, square. Old male, sixteen, eighteen years. Live
about twenty."

And who knows? Pandas might live here forever.
That's what I hoped, as I pictured again the best part
of the panda: his little tail
disappearing
into thick bamboo.

II *Garlands*

Along the path to the village
Foping to Sanguanmiao
swatches of white clematis bloom
like so many saucers in the wood.
Coming back, meet the handsome tracker
named Kun Hai. He smiles shyly,
a garland of white flowers
all around his head.

Next day across the river, trains
of cabbage white butterflies swirl,
males trailing females all through
the Asian air, the dogwood orchard,
three, four, five in a row. Then
a rollicking file of seven appears:
a garland of white butterflies
all around my head.

III The Enjoyment of Fishes

Headlines in a Chinese airline magazine section on "The 80's Generation: Will You Get Married This Year?": "If You Are the One, All on a Blind Date," "Marriage House: Test of Love," "Naked Wedding: Some Do, and Some Not," "Leftover Ladies: You Are Not a Fish; How Do You Know What Constitutes the Enjoyment of Fishes?"

As his friend asked Zhuangzi
on the River Hao so long ago,
"How could you know the joy
of the fishes? You are not a fish."
How *would* you know, when even
the fishes are mystified?

Maybe it's that golden glide over stone,
the otterish mingling of self and stream.
Attaining the top of the falls in spawn,
anticipation of broadcast milt.

Oh, we know the enjoyment of fish, all right,
in sushi, ceviche, and stew, pan-fried and smoked.
But not from the fishes' point of view,
much less that of the leftover ladies
of China.

JUST ABOUT

What I want to say is how mianthemum
and streamside violet and spring beauty and oxalis
cover the ground in April as thick as the mosses
and clubmosses and ferns jacket
the boughs of vine maples. How
the elderberry springs beneath the spruce
and the winter wren's many notes ride
the single chord of varied thrush. How
corydalis and salmonberry meet you
across the skinny bridge. What I want to say
is that all this ought to be enough
for anybody.

A MOON I DIDN'T SEE

for Patty

Was it low and red,
that moon you saw?
The color of a dull ache
long after a fall,
when it rose?

I didn't see it, so I don't know;
but I've seen moons that ached like that before.

Last night
another moon cruised
the ceiling of the fog, glanced
off the tin-roofed bridge
like a discus
thrown the old way,
skidding to a stop
in the river's moonglade.

I'd like to think of every moon
as mine
despite my absent eyes. Maybe
it's the moons you never see
that burn the deepest.

MOONRISE REDUX; OR, GONE FOR GOOD

I

Coming down from Sentinel, walking the few blocks home
past the notice on the telephone pole to watch
out for the neighborhood black bear, I notice
a bright light on the mountain: some beacon
I hadn't seen before? No! It's the moon! All full,
just cresting the ridge. I have missed the moment of rising.

II

And then it hits me: I could walk back
up the street, and the moon would drop again
beneath the climbing mountain's flank—I can get
the moonrise back, after all! Strange, at this late
date, that this should be news to me. So I backtrack,
and watch the moon rise thrice: that slow cool fire spreading
along the ridge until the silver rim appears: a hubcap in halogen,
every blade of bunchgrass, each sprig of chokecherry *etched*
against the Mare Tranquilitatis.

III

One month later I come outside to find
the next moon already up. But this time I know
exactly what to do. I have to walk fast,
but I catch it—just before it tops the summit
of Sentinel. Imagine! A chance to reclaim
what's lost, simply by adjusting your position
viz a viz the mountain, the moon.

IV

But in between these moons, fetched up
on the Maryland shore, I wake ungodly early to watch
the sun rise over the Atlantic. I hit the January beach
in time, turn my back on high-rise wall, and face

51

the sea, the scoters. Then two women catch
me in conversation until I turn, and *damn!*—there
it is, that mango fire, already limning the eastern curve.
Oh, I see most of the rise, that cerise tomato,
plopping up atop the wave, then yellow, then white
above the white shell sparkle of the beach. But I missed
the moment of ignition, that second when the sea gives
up the secret it doesn't know it knows:
that neither the ocean, nor the night, go on forever.

IN THE EXPERIMENTAL FOREST

And here is what the scientists see
but cannot say:

How the dogwood blossoms glow
against the black wet trunks of Douglas-fir,
how the skin of yew runs red in rain, the bark
of young vine maple green as skin of anole
in a hot southern wood.

The way evergreen violets erupt hot yellow
from the green magma of moss, and trilliums pink
out, pasting their petals to the waxy leather of salal.

The manner in which Douglas squirrels inscribe
the snow, and where they leave their middens.

Cascara's small tongues lapping the drip
as chorus frogs and winter wrens sound
the walls and depths of Lookout Creek. Pipsissewa
and bunchberry catching all the windthrow
winter can bring. All these things

may have adaptive value, for all we know.
Could generate data, yield understanding,
render the answers that poets may dream
but cannot write.

As last year's bracken rots beneath the new sword ferns
and varied thrushes whistle through spit,
I have faith
that somebody, somewhere,
surely knows
what to make of all this.

THE LIBRARIANS

There is a golden walnut tree outside
and a spider, dropping bit by bit on her way to work
like a lineman cinching down a cable, or a climber
rappelling. There are people
who do no harm from one day to the next. They spray
no poisons, drop no bombs, pave no meadows.

There are deep colors in this glass of ale,
and pools of liquid light on its surface
like ponds in Cumbria, or the second eyelids
of a seabird. There are people
who glow softly through the garish tumult. They make
no waves, launch no rockets, claim no fame.

Is this a genetic condition, to withstand
the no-tax morons, beat back the dunderheads, flail
the philistines with nothing more than the love of books
and reading? Or is it a matter of life and death?

The walnut will drop its leaves, and one of these nights
the spider will freeze. Books too will die,
they say. But don't believe it.
Not until the last librarian is gone
will I give up.

ATMOSPHERIC EFFECTS

I am too much of a skeptic to deny the possibility of anything.

—Thomas H. Huxley

I

Winter run down 101, past Protection Island,
sun comes out. Stirs the curdled fog,
steams the slick wet asphalt, turns
this gray-green tunnel through rainforest gloom
into boulevard of golden mist. Shimmers
over ditches thick with bracken,
running russet into dusk.

II

Out from under pallid sunset tatters
(bleached-out peach, dull bruised plum),
over Christmas lights of lone Montana ranch,
Cheshire cat with whitened teeth grins—
follows frozen tracks behind a train,
somewhere west of Havre.

III

Arcing over Willow Grove, rainbow frames
a passing vee. Twenty-two honkers cross
behind the gauzy bands like rabbits jumping
hula hoops. If only for the wink of an eye,
each gray goose turns Kodachrome.

IV

In a world where sun turns base fog into gold,
moon slips her traces to ride the rails, and
geese metamorphose into butterflies,
remind me now: what was it
you said was impossible?

THREE A.M. AT THE ALL-NIGHT LOGGING SHOW

Well, okay, not really all night. But this operation
starts up around two in the morning, shuts down early.
We're used to logging around here. The ragged
little mountain these guys are relieving of its alder
has been logged before; the next patch over
will go next year. The hill across the creek,
last cut before I came here in '78, will be felled
again in ten or fifteen years, I'd guess. For pulp—
this stuff I'm writing on. Loggers always go

to work early, stepping into their clammy, stagged-
off jeans about the time I turn in some nights. It's not
unusual to hear their whistle-bugs pipe up
at six, and the first loads grumble down the road
before dawn. But this logging in the middle of the night
is a new one on me: the sharp bleats of the bug
and the back-up beeps, the bass thrum of the cables
and higher whine of chokers; the diesel growl
of the cutter-loader, the scrape of the carriage,
and when they buck, the urgent howl
of chainsaws. The spotlights in the window.

They make a mess of sleep, the all-night loggers.
Out there working in the face-slapping rain,
the limb-whipping wind, the frigid fog. I shiver, pull
the blanket higher, turn back into my ragged dreams.

SHEETS ON THE LINE

February, after the rains,
before more rains,
the sun. A contrail slices off
a piece of blue sky. Snowdrops nod
among the brown dreck of last
year's montbretia. Late-lamented
honeybees come back from the dead
to probe their early nectar.

Sheets billow on the line,
wafting in the easterly like champing
sails of a brig held fast at anchor,
puffing out, slacking back,
shoving against the mainmast:
the granny pole that holds
the rigging in the middle,
eighteen wooden pins across.

The long flannel topsheet, doubled over,
then the fitted bottom, worn thin.
Two pillow cases, and one more
sheet of faded percale roses.
The matched set blows white,
bright with pink, red, yellow florets
on green leafy stalks snatched
from the mossy sward below. Blue
ashen dapples cross the cotton, melting
into shadows of their own collapse
as breeze-born crows fall and flap.
Twenty thousand wrinkles show
where our bodies have pressed
these sheets, and will press them afresh,
on a cold night, when the rain returns.

On days like this I see
why people take their lives
sometimes. Not because it's so bad,
but because it's so good,
quitting while they're ahead.

THE STARLING IN THE STOVE

Again the banging in the stove pipe that says
starling has taken chimney vent for nest-hole. Clangs
and batters, till you wonder how she can take it.
A butterfly net over an open hole in the wood stove
shows her the light. She finds her way out, into the net,
even blacker than before. In my hands, her feathers

greasy with soot, she cries bloody murder,
makes such a racket you'd think she'd gone
from the stovepipe into the fire. Once back
in the clean blue air, she bumps
a window, leaving a smudge. Then rockets
away, trading this bad dream for the open air.

"She's a cheap chimney sweep," you say,
and I say "Good," knowing another one
will be back next spring, to brush away
another winter's creosote.

TWO MORE BIRDS THAT DIDN'T MAKE IT

DOMINO EVENT MARRED BY DEAD BIRD
*Amsterdam. A Dutch television show claimed to have knocked down a chain of more than
4.1 million dominoes Friday in a new world record, but organizers conceded the event was
overshadowed by the earlier shooting of an errant sparrow. The sparrow was killed by an
exterminator with an air rifle on Monday after it knocked down 23,000 dominoes.*

—*Seattle Times*

I *The Starling in the Tulip*

And how did that small pink naked bird come to lie
within this tulip's mouth? Well, if you were walking
along a hot sidewalk in Denver, and you looked
down and saw a tiny nestling in your path; and if it had
a great wide yellow gape and wee, rosy buds of wings
without a feather; and if it lay dead, but perfect,
not yet trodden and smeared across the concrete.
And supposing there grew a Popsicle-pink tulip
a few feet away, petals spread to show
the paler pink within, sunsetting yellow at the base,
night-black, pollen-starred stamens pushing out
as if to say, "Welcome!"
Well, tell me—
what would you have done?

II *The Barn Swallow in the House*

"Do you think we live in a barn?' my father asked,
every time I left the door open. I guess that's what
the barn swallow thought. When you found it
in the living room, brought it out in your hands,
I thought it would leap into the air, fly away
in frantic relief, like the starlings we free
from the stove, when they tumble down the pipe.
It screamed, launched, circled twice, then crashed
to the lawn. After that, nothing got better. Tail tugged
right, head bent back, something broken. Shoebox;

60

water from a dropper. Drank, took neither moth
nor midge, then slept, maybe dreaming
of far, far flights. Started, looked around, waking
from good dream into bad life. Slept again.
Of course it was dead in the morning. Smoothed
the blue scissor-wings, stroked the rusty breast,
placed it to rest and rot in the plum grove beneath
mianthemum and bluebells. It was just one swallow,
of millions that vanish on each impossible round-trip.
But I didn't have to leave the damn door open, did I?

THE EVOLUTION OF THE GENUS *IRIS*

Those heat-heavy Denver afternoons
my grandmother brought me chocolate milk
in the shade of trumpet vines, then took her rest
inside. I waited for the cool of dusk to walk
the low rows of her irises, to suck
their outrageous scent—the yellow ones,
the lavender, the enigmatic brown called "root beer,"
the deepest purple. At dawn, Gram weeded
along the walk, divided the rhizomes
so my mother's garden might have them too.

Now, beside our kitchen wall in May,
the grapy petticoats of iris open, spill
their sweet stink onto the lilac-loaded air,
lay out their golden furry tongues to stroke
the bees into complicity with pollen.

These irises didn't come from Grammy's garden,
or from Mom's. Another woman laid them down,
broke them up, left them here for us. Yet they are
the same irises. Their roots run,
like the wild iris of these hills, back
to the original tuber. And when
their extravagant blooms fold
in upon themselves and rot,
even as the next night-purple spear unfurls,
their ink bleeds from the same deep well.

RARE BEARS

It's the rarest bear in the world, the white Kermode of British Columbia.

—Elaine Glusac, *Islands Magazine*

Maybe so. But it cannot be a common honor,
spending time with panda and koala
in the wild,
only weeks apart. Their

living roundnesses of hope
and hair and scratching claw
(panda, bear all right, but pied
like no other; koala, just
a so-called bear, marsupial in fact,
like all its Ozzie friends), both curled
into their habitats of deep bamboo and gum.

It's a lucky man who comes through life
as richly graced as this;
a lucky world, where animals
like these can even be imagined,
much less seen. And if

they should pass from the scene
someday, as they surely will,
but I mean, too soon?

Then I'd have to ask: what
kind of luck is this, that renders our days
so rich in bears,
then strips the world of all
that matters most?

CANCER INCANTATION

O you sand-smashing waves
you bone-picking buzzards
O otters cracking sculpin skulls and scales
Kingfisher driving away your rival
with spear of beak and rattle of life
O coyote prizing voles from violet earth
You elk who hoof hard steeps to duff
O mussel-cruncher seal
O beaver bringer-down of tree
Spruce who breaks old rock with root
Sun who gobbles up each day
Moon, consumer of the night
Alder wolfing naked slope
You deer who pluck the bursting twig
Peregrine who takes the duck in flight
O salmon thrashing waterfall and nymph
Eagle snagging jack and cutthroat
O you cliff unmaking surf and
clam-unclasping, clutching gull
You raven, crow and jay who steal
the eggs that want to hatch and fledge:

Wave and vulture, seal and otter,
kingfisher, beaver, coyote and crow,
salmon, eagle, elk and jay,
sun and moon and spruce and alder,
deer and falcon, gull and raven,
all you who kill to eat and eat to live:
come in, come in, come in—

Kill this cancer! Eat it!
Live long and thrive.

THE LAST RIDE OF SUMMER

All summer long, Dear, we've ridden
these ferries across the northern Sound—
Anacortes to Friday Harbor and back. We came
to see what butterflies fly on San Juan Island:
over the grasslands, through the forest, along
the bluffs, above the beach and driftwood.
Calling on the lupine, nettle, and strawberry,
the gumweed, the goldenrod, pearly everlasting;
the bramble, beach pea, and beach radish,
ocean spray, dogwood, and oak. There were
the island marbles, of course, rediscovered
for us; how we found them in the peppergrass
and mustard. The ringlets, coppers, and skippers,
the swallowtails,
the fritillary you saw here once before. Finally,
in September . . . but that's this time, my love!
What do you suppose will be on the wing?
The sun is on our side.

THE GIRL WITH THE COCKLEBURS IN HER HAIR

We were talking about how children don't
get out any more. She showed me
her daughter on her cell phone:
big pout, and four big burs
caught up in her hair.
That girl, I said, is
going to be
okay.

in Latin, "tailed frog" to you and me. Only
one of its clan in the whole New World:
nearest kin, New Zealand. Frequents
such rivers as give Cascades their
name, fast and clean. Adults have
no ears or voice: why chorus in
noisy water? The male has a
penis in place of mere cloaca:
false, so called, but works,
so sperms aren't flushed
away. Tailed tadpoles
have suckers to cling
in rushing streams.
Saw one today in
Lookout Creek!
Been looking
hard, these
forty-five
years.

THE ELK COME

Just days ago, Celia camped in this meadow.
Now fifty or sixty elk chomp grass, trample
the corn lilies, lie in moonlight; ruminate
all 'round where Celia's tent so lately stood.

At dinner comes the hoarse and high-pitched wheedle
and roar that marks the bugling bull, keeping
his harem together, keeping other males in place,
as corn lily crispens and summer starts back down.

Later, with chocolate, tea, and apricots, we watch
(from under mantle-glow) a hundred head go crunch!
crunch! on gravel road, then jump, or shove,
or just ignore the twanging fence.

In moonbeams like the sun they are, elk spook
into brief stampede. Soon stilled, they huff
and stamp, turn about, lie down—just fifty yards
away across split-rail and barbed wire.

We listen for an hour more, afraid to wreck
this peaceable kingdom of bugle, huff, and chew.
Small owl slides by, back and forth, as I make out
antlers, dark shoulders, all those big white butts.

Cold and sleepy, we turn in. Wapiti pay
no mind at all. Early morning, rise and go. I walk
down to see what all that grinding's wrought:
pellets everywhere, blue butterflies come to sip.

Bear sign shows in dried mud, chickarees, chipmunks,
ground squirrels abound. White-tail faces off
at twenty feet and stamps. All that's left of cow and calf,
of old bull's hoot and huff and grunt: their beds lie flat,

and the meadow smells of piss and hay, like a stable.

NOTES FROM THE EDGE OF THE KNOWN WORLD

When winter wren and varied thrush break into April voices
and elderberry branches crack and thrust, and Sitka spruce and
caws of crow and wild waves all slap on ocean shore, this
small black beetle jaws a crumb and smaller scarlet mite roves
over needled dirt to somewhere we will never see, as sword
fern rots upon its ancient mound and fiddleheads unfurl. When
sorrel triplets burst upon the guileless scene and moss-hung
branches point a way through trackless wood, where puma sinks
its teeth in throat of deer who gives its life unwillingly but has
no choice.

When somewhere on the other side of time and whirling world
beside some withered waterhole a warthog coughs
and baboon flashes scarlet rump and grimace blue and toothy
at the other males, at swollen gravid female, at lioness who charges,
then withdraws behind the yellow grass. Then polar bears on permafrost
and skuas over tundra sedge will take whatever sustenance
the day affords, then sleep, and sleep, and sleep some more despite
the midnight sun. As in the forest gloom the lichen hangs
and sways above the snailish stream and mushrooms crowd
the mossy bank where hemlocks screen the sunlight from the silage
of the slugs and slime, of molds and time, where waterbears
and woodlice roam, bacteria and nematodes make way
among the great and fleshy entrails of the world.

And what about the turquoise-manteled giant clam cemented
in the coral reef beneath antipodean skies, the urchins dragging
spines across the limey bottoms, poking holes in waterbags to make
the ocean new for every life on every tide? Or clouds that drop
their shadows on the desert floor, that parking lot for tortoises,
where cactus reaches out for gods it never knew or needed?
Flash-floods scrape away whatever luck the horned toad
ever had. Which isn't much, it seems,

until you think of otter clamped in orca's gape
or flank of desert oryx running red beneath the claws of leopard,
every desiccated leaf and flower folded in upon itself, until
you think of ants and worms and voles and frogs in tractor ruts
or salmon smolts in heron's bill. Until you think of this great ape,
the one that stands upright and poses every question ever asked,
in such a world where everything that grows breaks down
and down, and down, then grows, and grows and grows,
and grows again.

ACKNOWLEDGMENTS

Thanks attend the editors of the following magazines and books where many of these poems first appeared, often in somewhat different form:

Bear Essential: "Life and Death in Yellowstone"

Camas: "The Banana Slug on the Totem Pole," "Horseback at Dawn," "Moonlight Redux; or, Gone for Good"

Convolvulus: "The Grief of Thrushes," "After Birth"

From the Lost Corner: "Hearth"

Hawk and Handsaw: "The Enjoyment of Fishes"

High Desert Journal: "Early Morning in Wyoming," "The Girl with the Cockleburs in Her Hair"

Isle: "Botany Lesson: Cleome," "Lullaby for Pattiann," "Sheets on the Line"

Isotope: "Two Haiku from Ryukyu" (with Gary Snyder)

Moon City Review: "Pink Pavements," "True Story," "In the Experimental Forest"

North American Review : "Evolution of the Genus *Iris*"

Portland: "Silage," "The Butterflies of Billy Meadows"

Rain: "The Last Ride of Summer," "Dancing Pants," "Blues," "The Goats of Tajikistan," "Life Can Be Like This Sometimes," "Three A.M. at the All-Night Logging Show," "Atmospheric Effects," "Gulls at Rest"

Salal: "Two More Birds That Didn't Make It," "All Fall Down," "News Item"

Scarabogram: "Releasing the Horseflies," "Dip-Tych"

Terrain.org: "*Ascaphus truei*"

Wamka: "Coyote, Hit"

Whole Terrain: "Notes from the Edge of the Known World" (in part); (an audio version of "Notes from the Edge of the Known World, read by the author with acoustic guitar composition written and performed by Krist Novoselic, appears at http://graysrivergrange.org/?page_id=105 and at http://www.youtube.com/watch?v=OoPSHtirAbs)

BOOKS AND CHAPBOOKS

Letting the Flies Out (chapbook, Fishtrap, Inc., 2nd & 3rd editions, New Riverside Press): "The Elk Come," "The Butterflies of Billy Meadows," "Going Down Again," "Haiku for a Beetle with Spiderwebs on its Antennae," "Releasing the Horseflies,' "Dip-tych," "The Pulaski on the Flagpole"

Markings on a Page (chapbook, Peasandcues Press): "The Librarians"

Matter & Spirit (chapbook, Fishtrap, Inc.): "Going Down Again" and "Haiku for a Beetle with Spiderwebs on its Antennae"

Moon Museum (chapbook, Heartbreak Press): "A Moon I Didn't See"

Three lucky writing residencies were crucial to the development of this book, and I am deeply grateful for them: the Sitka Center for Art and Ecology, Otis, Oregon; Werner Writing Residency at Billy Meadows, Blue Mountains, Oregon, thanks to Ann Werner and Fishtrap, Inc.; and a New Riverside Residency, Willapa Hills, Washington.

My dear ten-year writing group (Greg Darms, Susan Holway, Brian Harrison, John Indermark, Diane Matthews, Brian Pentilla, Patricia Staton Thomas, Jenelle Varila, Lorne Wirkkala) read, critiqued, jawboned, and much improved many of these poems in early drafts. Others arose or evolved under the influence of a fine poetry group at Utah State University: Star Coulbrooke, Anne Shifrer, Brock Dethier, Shanan Ballam, Adrienne Platero, Robb Kunz, Charles Cuthbertson, and Cynthia Leyson. Nate McKeen hooked me up with *North American Review.*

Kind thanks to Gary Snyder, for his big help with "The Pulaski on the Flagpole" and "Two Haiku from Ryukyu," his permission to reprint the latter here, and for his life-long example. Further high thanks to Ko Un, Sang-Wha Lee, Chris Cokinos, Leslie Brown, Katsunori Yamazato, and Scott Slovic for facilitating "Two Haiku from Ryukyu." I owe huge thanks to Krist Novoselic for inspiring "Notes from the Edge of the Known World" with his brilliant guitar song for it.

Good friends who have swapped poems and encouragement include Barbara Drake, Alice Derry, Pattiann Rogers, Alison Deming, Jane Hirschfield, Holly Hughes, Tim McNulty, Carolyn Maddux, Charles Goodrich, Joe Green, Sam Green, Ann Spiers, Bill Yake, Jim Bertolino, Anita Boyle, Brian Doyle, Derrick Sheffield, David Taylor, John Lane, Kim Stafford, Ursula LeGuin, Saul Weisberg, Kristin Berger, Ellen Waterston, Clem Starck, Charles Finn, Chris Cokinos, John Daniel, Maya Jewel Zeller, Irene Martin, David Campiche, Jim Dott, Nancy Cook, Florence Sage, John Ciminello, Luke Johnson, Henry Hughes, Gary Cummisk, Wenonah Sharpe, Hannah Fries, Barbara Deutsch, and the late Robert Sund, the only person who came to my first reading, in LaConner, Washington; we just sat by the water and traded poems and tales all the long warm afternoon.

Thanks with all my heart to Christine Holbert, publisher and designer of Lost Horse Press, for bringing my Iris so beautifully to bloom; to Christopher Howell and Henry Hughes for their astute review and suggestions; to artist Lexie Sundell for her lovely and stunning cover painting, and to Benj Drummond for his author's photo.

And especially and always, my ever-loving thanks to Thea Linnaea Pyle, the reason for it all. I shall miss her beyond all expression.